Little Walks

A guide to walks on the
Great Allegheny Passage
& connecting trails
in the Pittsburgh Area

Yvonne Merrill
AE Richardson
& Mary Shaw

A project of the
Allegheny Trail Alliance
www.atatrail.org

Credits

Copyright © 2003 Allegheny Trail Alliance
Printed in United States of America
ISBN   0-9727324-0-3
Published by Great Allegheny Press, an imprint of
Shaw-Weil Associates
419 College Avenue, Greensburg, PA 15601
First edition. First printing, May 2003.

Photos

Photos were taken by Yvonne Merrill, unless otherwise noted.

Acknowledgements

This book was produced by the Allegheny Trail Alliance (ATA) with financial support from the Jewish Healthcare Foundation and Bill Novelli, Executive Director and CEO of AARP, who kindly designated a portion of his 2003 Porter Prize to ATA's older adult outreach program. Thanks to Shaw-Weil Associates for permission to use driving directions from *FreeWheeling Easy in Western Pennsylvania,* Bill Metzger for maps, Sandra Finley and Roy Weil for wordsmithing, and trail organizations for providing information.

Introduction

This little book presents a dozen great little trips for casual walks on the trails of the Great Allegheny Passage in Allegheny and northern Washington Counties with a few more on nearby trails. Each trip has something special to see or experience and a good place to park your car. Most have public transportation, drinking water, rest rooms, and a place to sit down for a snack. Some have bike rentals and restaurants.

These great little walks are mostly on former railroad beds that have been converted to walking and biking trails and are open to the public for non-motorized activity, making safe and pleasant walks. Some of these walks include a few street crossings, but they are limited.

These trails are friendly public community trails, with good walking surfaces. A few are paved and suitable for in-line skating. They are nearly level, with very few—and very short—hills making most of them wheelchair accessible. You will find most of the trails on average are 8-12 feet wide, well marked, and easy to find. And once you are on them, it's pretty tough to get lost. They are great places to get out for a walk, take the kids biking, watch birds, walk the dog, meet people, and enjoy the scenic beauty of southwestern Pennsylvania. All you need are good walking shoes, comfortable clothing, and this book.

Table of Contents

Disclaimer: On Safety, Judgment, & Personal Responsibility

Trail activities have intrinsic risks, for which you must assume responsibility. We cannot be responsible for mishaps or problems you encounter on your trip. Ultimately, the quality of your experience depends on your own use of common sense and good judgment.

We have made a diligent effort to present accurate descriptions and to confirm trail conditions and services. However, weather, wear, construction, vandalism, and other forces can alter conditions, erode trail surfaces, create obstacles, or even close trails. Businesses can close or change management, and quality may change as a result. Therefore we cannot be responsible for discrepancies between these descriptions and actual conditions. If you do encounter any discrepancies, let us know.

Family time on the Passage. By Anthony Marich Jr.

Chart of Walks

Walk	Page #	Total Distance	Surface
1. Around the Island	12	1.5-mile loop	packed stone
2. Forts & Sports	16	4.0-mile loop	concrete, stone, & brick
3. Walkway East	20	5.3 miles	asphalt
4. Take a Walk on the South Side	24	1.5 & 3.8 miles	asphalt & crushed limestone
5. Wilderness in the City	28	2.8 miles	asphalt
6. Steel Valley Promenade	32	2.3 miles	crushed stone
7. Sweet Enlow	36	3.8 miles	crushed stone
8. Walker's Mile	40	4.6 miles	crushed stone
9. National Tunnel	44	2.2 miles	crushed stone
10. Pace Peters	48	6.4 miles	asphalt
11. Haunting Beauty	52	2.3 miles	crushed stone, mulch, gravel, dirt
12. Old Towns & New Prairies	56	5.8 & 9.2 miles	crushed stone

Bus #	Rentals	Drinking Water	Public Toilet	Food
1F, 1B	no	vending machine	no	yes
all 61, 71, T	no	yes	yes	yes
lots & T	bike & skate	yes	yes	yes
51A, 51C	no	no	yes	yes
none	no	no	no	no
55D, 56E 59U	no	yes	yes	yes
26E, 28E	no	yes	yes	yes
33F	no	no	yes	yes
none	no	yes	yes	yes
none	no	no	yes	yes
60A	bike	yes	yes	yes
none	no	yes	yes	yes

Foreword

In 1948, when the Graduate School of Public Health (GSPH) was formed, Pittsburgh's biggest health challenges were due to its smoky industries.

Today, our biggest health challenges are due to our aging population, the second oldest in America. Just as fifty years ago the GSPH provided the scientific information that was instrumental in protecting the public from air pollution, today we are providing the scientific information that provides the basis for healthy aging.

Some of the clearest messages from our research at the Center for Healthy Aging are the importance of walking to health, and the value of trails and other attractive and convenient walkways to promoting health. Through its activities supporting the development and use of walking trails, the Allegheny Trail Alliance is a model of effective public health promotion.

Bernard D. Goldstein, M.D.
Dean of the University of Pittsburgh
Graduate School of Public Health

Using This Book

Each walk description includes a narrative of the walk, driving directions, parking, public transportation information, and a map.

Amenities such as portable toilets, public phones, drinking fountains, and places for food and drink are noted in the narrative or on the map. Keep in mind that water is sometimes shut off in colder seasons and portable toilets may not have tissue or may even be removed.

The overview map inside the back cover shows where each walk is located in and around Pittsburgh. The contacts and websites listed at the end of this book (pages 61-63) are accurate as of April 2003 and can provide updates and more detailed information.

Authors' Note

If you are arriving via public transportation, check with the Port Authority of Allegheny County for current route and schedule information (412-442-2000 or www.portauthority.org). If you're driving, check with PennDOT for road detours, especially in downtown Pittsburgh (412-429-5000 or www.epenndot.com)

Using The Maps

The maps show each walk with icons for parking, drinking water, restroom or portable toilets, points of interest, major roadways, and nearby vendors.

Most of these walks start at trail access areas and are not loops. Therefore, you must turn around and head back the same way you came to complete the walk.

From the maps you will see that often the trail continues beyond the described walk. These walks are on sections of a larger trail system called the Great Allegheny Passage, which is over 200 miles long. For more information on the Great Allegheny Passage, see page 60 or http://www.atatrail.org.

Key to Symbols

Listed with each walk are symbols that indicate special features of that given trail. For instance, the symbol for bikes means that bikes are permitted on that trail. The symbol for wheelchair means that use of a wheelchair is possible. *The trail surface can be hard or soft depending on weather conditions, so keep this in mind if you plan to use wheelchairs, tricycles, or walking aids.*

The legend for symbols is on the last page (64) of this book.

Using The Trails
What to Take
Once you choose your walk and read the narrative, you can decide what you will need to take with you. Most of these are short walks and no special equipment is needed other than comfortable shoes and clothing—and this book.

Consider bringing these items with you:

Identification	Camera
Pedometer	Water
Snacks	Wipes
Sunscreen & Hat	Cell Phone*
Change for Phones & Vending Machines	

Cell phones should work on all of the walks listed in this book.

Courtesy
Walk on the right. Be observant. When there's other traffic, walk single file. Listen for "on your left," which means that a bike is about to pass. It is not necessary to leave the trail, but it is courteous to move to the right-hand edge. On all of these trails, dogs must be leashed and proper clean-up of waste is required.

Safety
Be sensible. As with any trip, *let friends know where and when you're going. Be prepared for minor first aid,* such as bug bites and blisters.

> **Authors' Note**
> Before embarking on any walk, be sure your shoes fit properly: snug at heel and roomy at the toes.

#1 Around the Island
Washington's Landing, North Shore

Location: City of Pittsburgh, Allegheny County
Length: 1.5-mile loop
Surface: packed stone
Slope: mostly flat with slight hills, 4 ft. wide, best for walking. Not recommended for wheelchair use.

Select this walk to visit an island that symbolizes the city's ability to transform itself from a dirty, industrial empire to a beautiful, livable community. Once known as Herr's Island, Washington's Landing is rich with history. It has been the site of everything from oil refineries to stock-yards to a garbage dump. Though condemned as a contaminated brownfield site in the 1970s, it was reclaimed in the 1990s for housing, offices, a marina, a park, and river trails.

The Walk

Starting at the parking lot under the 31st Street Bridge, use the sidewalk to walk past office buildings to the **Three Rivers Rowing Boat House**. Just past the Boat House, the sidewalk surface changes to packed stone. The back channel area you're entering is very peaceful, unlike the busy main channel. Ornamental grasses dot the trail side and mature trees provide ample shade. Go past the little **stone amphitheater** to reach a small park at the north end of the island.

Photo compliments of The Pittsburgh Post Gazette

You may choose to walk down the 46 steps leading to the river and this popular **fishing spot** where you can see the 40th Street Bridge marked **"Washington's Crossing,"** where George Washington crossed in 1753.

When you leave the park, continue around the island toward the main channel. After this, the trail goes through the marina and passes Troll's Restaurant. Continue along the path beside the condos and the river to the end of the island. Here, you'll see a bridge that links Washington's Landing to the **North Shore Trail**. To return to your car, go back a short distance and walk between the condos. Follow Waterfront Street back to the parking lot.

Amenities
Vending machines dispensing water and soft drinks can be found at the marina. The only restroom, for customers, is at Troll's Restaurant. There are two public phones, one in front of

the Boat House (300 Waterfront Drive) and the other at Troll's just outside the restroom.

Authors' Note
This beautiful little island is a must-see. Take time to read the signs along the way that interpret and explain the island's history.

Getting There
By Public Transit: The nearest bus stop is at the 31st Street Bridge and River Avenue. Buses are the 1F Millvale and 1B Mount Royal. Only commuter buses run to the island. Check with the Port Authority for current schedules: 412-442-2000.

By Car: From Downtown Pittsburgh, take I-579N (Veteran's Bridge), merge onto PA-28N toward Etna, 1.3 miles. Turn right onto 31st Street Bridge, 0.1 miles. Turn right onto River Avenue, 0.1 miles. Turn left onto 30th Street Bridge, 0.1 miles. The 30th Street Bridge becomes Waterfront Drive, where you will find parking.

From Pittsburgh's North Shore: Follow East Ohio Street/PA-28N toward Etna, 1.33 miles past I-579. Proceed as above.

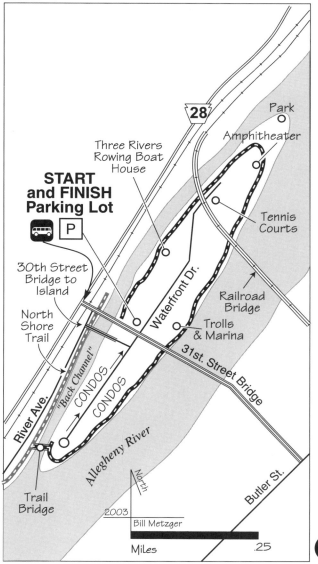

START and FINISH Parking Lot

30th Street Bridge to Island

North Shore Trail

Three Rivers Rowing Boat House

Park

Amphitheater

Tennis Courts

Waterfront Dr.

Railroad Bridge

Trolls & Marina

31st. Street Bridge

Butler St.

River Ave.

"Back Channel"

CONDOS

CONDOS

Allegheny River

Trail Bridge

North

2003

Bill Metzger

Miles

.25

#2 Forts & Sports
Pittsburgh's Point & Allegheny Shore

Location: Point State Park, Allegheny River North & South Shores, Allegheny County
Length: 4-mile loop
Surface: concrete, stone, and brick
Slope: level, some ramps

Select this walk on the Three Rivers Heritage Trail to visit Fort Pitt at the Point, mingle with people headed for a ball game, get great views of downtown Pittsburgh from across the Allegheny River, and visit the fountains or the sculpture park.

The Walk

Start at Point State Park where the **Fort Pitt Museum** interprets the strategic importance of the Forks of the Ohio River during the French and Indian War.

Enjoy the **fountain** at the point, then head to the **Fort Duquesne Bridge** at the northeast corner of the park. Cross the Allegheny River using the pedestrian walkway on the bridge.

At the end of the walkway, go left along the esplanade to check out **Heinz Field**, the home of Steeler football. You may cross the street to the **Carnegie Science Center** and UPMC Sports Works where you'll find the submarine

USS Requin on display. This is your turn-around point; return to the esplanade beside the river.

Water steps and PNC Park, North Shore

On your way back, with the river on your right, head for the area between the two stadiums. Here you'll find the Vietnam Veteran's Monument, Korean War Memorial, pedestrian pier, and **water steps**.

Continue past PNC Park; on either side of the 6th Street Bridge you'll find a path on your left leading up to street level, **PNC Park**, and **restaurants**. This is a great place to stop for food and drink.

Return to the trail and continue in the same direction past a colorful **sculpture garden** and the architecturally intriguing **Alcoa Building**. In front of the Alcoa Building, take the ramp up to the 7th Street Bridge to cross the Allegheny River, returning to the city side, then descend to river level on the walkway with the river on your right. Return to your start place, Point State Park, along the south shore side of the Allegheny River.

Amenities

A public phone, vending machines, and restroom facilities (seasonal) are at Point State Park. There are plenty of restaurants, coffee shops, ice cream shops, and pizza places near PNC Park and Sixth Street. Emergency phones are located between the two stadiums.

Getting There

By Public Transit: Transit stops at Gateway Center are within two blocks of Point State Park. All 61 and 71 buses stop along Liberty Avenue. The Light Rail Transit ("T") Gateway Center stop is at Stanwix Street and Forbes Avenue, cross to Liberty Avenue, walk left, two blocks to Point State Park. From other transit stops, look for signs directing you to Point State Park. Check with the Port Authority for current schedules: 412-442-2000.

By Car: Located at the tip of Pittsburgh's Golden Triangle, Point State Park is accessible from the East by I-376 and Stanwix Street, West by I-279 and Grant Street, North by PA-8, and south by PA-51 to the Liberty Tunnel and across the Liberty Bridge. Parking is plentiful at public parking lots.

Authors' Note
This walk is great for history buffs. You'll be in the places where forts once stood and stadiums now tower, together outlining Pittsburgh's place in history. Don't forget your camera!

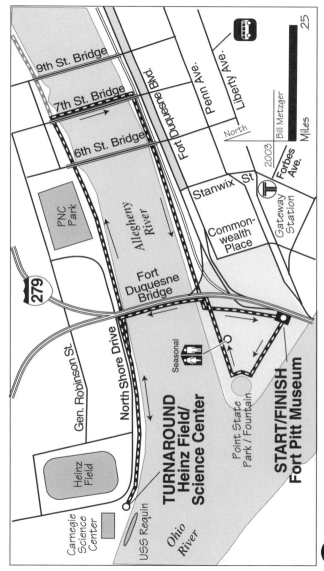

9th St. Bridge

7th St. Bridge

6th St. Bridge

Penn Ave.

Liberty Ave.

.25

Fort Duquesne Blvd.

North

Bill Metzger

Miles

2003

Forbes Ave.

Stanwix St

Gateway Station

Common-wealth Place

Allegheny River

PNC Park

279

Fort Duquesne Bridge

Gen. Robinson St.

North Shore Drive

Seasonal

TURNAROUND
Heinz Field/
Science Center

Point State Park / Fountain

START/FINISH
Fort Pitt Museum

Heinz Field

Carnegie Science Center

USS Requin

Ohio River

2 Forts and Sports

#3 Walkway East: Eliza Furnace
Grant Street to Greenfield

Location: City of Pittsburgh, Allegheny County
Length: 5.3-mile round-trip
Surface: parallel trails of asphalt and crushed stone
Slope: level

Select this sunny walk for its diverse urban atmosphere. The buzz of the city gives way to the open feel of modern industry and great views of the Monongahela River. This trail is 2.6 miles of smooth asphalt, a favorite of inline skaters, families with small children on bikes, and those using wheelchairs and walking aids. This section of the Three Rivers Heritage Trail connects downtown and Greenfield, and parallels the north shore of the Monongahela River and the Parkway East (I-376).

The Walk

Start your walk behind the new **PNC Firstside Center** at Grant Street and First Avenue. To do so, follow PNC's sidewalk and head toward the river and behind the building. Once on the trail, you'll pass between the First Avenue Garage and **Golden Triangle Bike Rental**, where you can rent skates and bikes and buy snacks and beverages. You'll pass under bridges, between highways, and around overpasses decorated in urban art. At rush hour you'll enjoy going faster than the traffic. Remember to keep your eyes open for fast-moving bike commuters who

Eliza Furnace Trail. By Mary Shaw

choose to use this trail instead of the Parkway.

Along your walk, you'll find **interpretive exhibits** explaining nearby landmarks and city heritage. You'll get **great views** of the growing Pittsburgh Technology Center and the Monongahela River. When you get to the parking lot at the Greenfield end, turn around and enjoy the views of downtown as you return.

Amenities

At the First Avenue end of the trail, a drinking fountain, snacks, and bike and skate rentals are available from the Golden Triangle Bike Shop under the Light Rail Transit Bridge. You are also within blocks of many eating establishments. The First Avenue Garage has restrooms, drinking fountains, and phones. The Second Avenue Parking Plaza has a portable toilet. Additionally, the Greenfield Parking Lot has a drinking fountain and portable toilet. Five blocks from the Greenfield end of the trail is

> **Authors' Note**
> When you return to Grant Street, go around the PNC Firstside building to the front to see if the fountain is running. It's one of the most intriguing fountains in town!

Big Jim's Restaurant & Bar (201 Saline Street). If you follow the arrows on the pavement for Panther Hollow, they will lead you to Big Jim's.

Getting There
By Public Transit: Take the Light Rail Transit ("T") to the First Avenue stop and walk down to ground level. Plenty of buses stop at Grant Street and Forbes Avenue or Grant Street and Fifth Avenue. Check with the Port Authority for current schedules: 412-442-2000.

By Car: This walk is easily accessible from Grant Street, Ross Street, First Avenue, Second Avenue, the Boulevard of the Allies, and I-376 Parkway East. From the Parkway, take Exit 1-C, Grant Street, at the 2nd traffic light make a right onto First Avenue and park in the First Avenue Garage. Pick up the trail between the parking garage and the Parkway. Or walk a half block towards Grant Street and pick up the trail by the PNC Firstside Building.

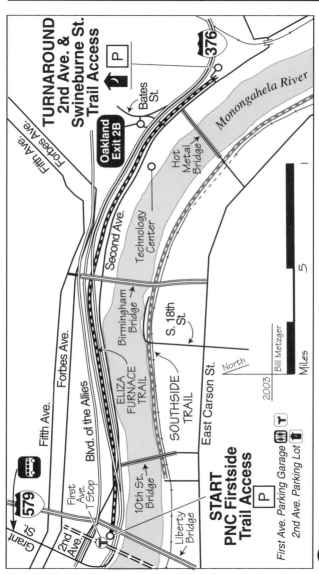

TURNAROUND 2nd Ave. & Swineburne St. Trail Access

376

Bates St.

Monongahela River

Oakland Exit 2B

Hot Metal Bridge

Second Ave.

Technology Center

Forbes Ave.

Fifth Ave.

Birmingham Bridge

S. 18th St.

Forbes Ave.

Fifth Ave.

Blvd. of the Allies

ELIZA FURNACE TRAIL

SOUTHSIDE TRAIL

East Carson St.

North

2003   Bill Metzger

5

Miles

First Ave. T Stop

579

Grant St.

2nd Ave.

10th St. Bridge

Liberty Bridge

START PNC Firstside Trail Access

First Ave. Parking Garage

2nd Ave. Parking Lot

❸ **Walkway East**

#4 Take a Walk on the South Side
Monongahela South Shore

Location: South Side, Pittsburgh, Allegheny County
Length: 1.5-mile round-trip and 3.8-mile round-trip
Surface: asphalt (with parallel crushed stone trail in parts)
Slope: nearly level

Select these walks on the Three Rivers Heritage Trail to enjoy river front views of the Pittsburgh skyline, which provides a perfect backdrop for a shore-side stroll. Picnic tables, benches, a boat launch, and interpretive exhibits along the banks make it a great place to take friends and family or out-of-town guests to show off the city.

The Shorter Walk

Starting at the parking lot at the South Side Riverfront Park, the trail runs in both directions along the river. The shorter walk (1.5 miles) is toward the left as you face the river. Follow the sidewalk to 18th Street; the trail picks up between the railroad tracks and the river. Overhanging trees shade this beautiful section of the trail where you'll see nice views of the **Pittsburgh skyline**. Interpretive exhibits along the way give highlights of the city's history in the steel and glass industries, railroad lines, canal system, and immigrant workers. The trail ends at 9th Street by the **Equitable Gas Plant**. Turn around here and trace your steps back to the parking lot.

The Longer Walk

For a longer walk, turn right from the parking lot as you face the river. Follow the trail south from the upper-level parking lot under the Birmingham Bridge. *Caution! Do not confuse the trail with the sidewalk in the park that runs closer to the river.* Use caution crossing Hot Metal Street. At 0.9 miles, look for the **sunken barge** at the site of the former **LTV Steel Plant**. You can spot some well-known Pittsburgh landmarks from here: the **Cathedral of Learning**, **USX Tower**, **Parkway**, and **Mellon Building** to name a few. If you like art, stop to see the 10' x 60' **mural** in the lobby of the Steeler/ UPMC Sports com-plex. Just beyond the practice stadiums, at 1.3 miles, the parallel trail and landscaping end. At 1.9 miles, near Becks Run Road, anoth-er gorgeous

10th St. Bridge & Duquesne University

> **Authors' Note**
> An Industrial Garden of trail art is located near Hot Metal Street; slag mounds, a curving steel bench and a massive Steel Workers Monument commemorate the railroads and steel industry.

overlook graces the trail side along this newest section. Although the trail continues for another 1.5 miles, this is a good place to turn back to complete a 3.8-mile round-trip.

Amenities

At South Side Riverfront Park you will find ample free parking, portable toilets, benches, picnic tables, a pay phone, and a boat-launching ramp. Here you're only two blocks from the South Side's main street, East Carson Street, where you will find many fine restaurants, pubs, eateries, and shopping.

Getting There

By Public Transit: Take the 51A or 51C bus to 18th Street and East Carson. Follow South 18th Street to Riverfront Park. Check with the Port Authority for current schedules: 412-442-2000.

By Car: You can reach the South Side via the Smithfield Street Bridge (left onto East Carson Street), 10th Street Bridge (two blocks, left onto East Carson Street) or Birmingham Bridge (right onto East Carson Street). From East Carson Street, turn toward the river on South 18th Street and follow to South Side Riverfront Park.

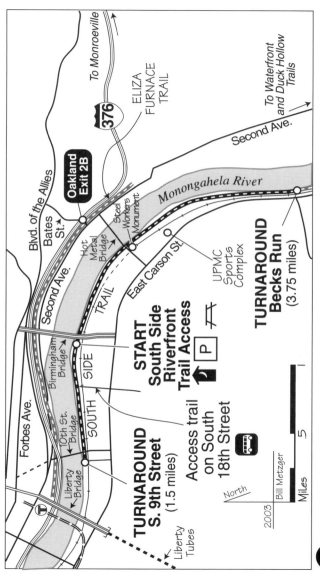

4 Take a Walk on the South Side

#5 Wilderness in the City
Duck Hollow

Location: Squirrel Hill, City of Pittsburgh, Allegheny County
Length: 2.8-mile round-trip
Surface: asphalt
Slope: nearly level, slightly undulating

Select this walk to experience near-wilderness in the city and views of The Waterfront in Homestead across the Monongahela River. This walk, on a shady trail surfaced in asphalt, blends Pittsburgh's industrial past and commercial present for an interesting visual mix in a quiet, isolated woodland setting. Officially called the Upper Monongahela Trail, this trail is known among the locals as Duck Hollow; it is part of the Three Rivers Heritage Trail and will eventually connect with Nine Mile Run, leading into Frick Park.

The Walk

As you face the river, **The Waterfront** lies directly across the river. The trail to your right gently winds between river and railroad, passing under the hulking shadow of the **Homestead Grays/High Level Bridge.** Mulched areas provide sunlit rest spots with views of commercial tugs and pleasure boats, common along this section of river. Towering smokestacks of the former **US Steel**

Homestead Works are visible across the river. At 0.9 miles, the skeletal remains of a **river-rail terminal** rust away. Here, coal

Curved trestle at 1.3 miles of this walk

was transferred from rail cars to barges for shipment down river. The trail then opens up to a nice view of **Sandcastle Water Park** as you pass under an active **railroad trestle**. At 1.4 miles, just short of the Glenwood Bridge, the trail ends at a chain link fence. Turn around to complete a 2.8-mile walk.

Amenities

At Duck Hollow, you'll find ample free parking, trash receptacles and little else. The closest restaurant is Wendy's, over half a mile up the hill at 4524 Browns Hill Road. Other additional restrooms, drinking water, public phones, shopping, and restaurants are a short drive across the Homestead Grays/High Level Bridge at The Waterfront's Town Square.

Getting There

By Public Transit: Though buses do stop at Browns Hill Road and Old Browns Hill, a very steep 0.5-mile walk on this dead-end road down the hill to the trail make it unadvisable.

By Car: From I-376 (Parkway East), take Exit 5 (Squirrel Hill/ Homestead), follow signs for Homestead. Cross Hazelwood Avenue, stay straight onto Browns Hill Road, make left onto Old Browns Hill Road, continue 0.5 miles down the hill, bear right into the parking lot.

From Homestead, cross the Homestead Grays/ High Level Bridge toward Squirrel Hill, make a right at the first traffic light onto Old Browns Hill Road, continue 0.5 miles down the hill, bear right into the parking lot.

Authors' Note
When you return from your walk, you may choose to see more by crossing the bridge on the far end of the parking lot, and bearing left. You'll see the small village of Duck Hollow with well-kept homes huddled against a slag pile, another remnant of the industrial age. Isolated from the rest of the world, a peaceful aura surrounds this tiny neighborhood of picket fences and colorful gardens.

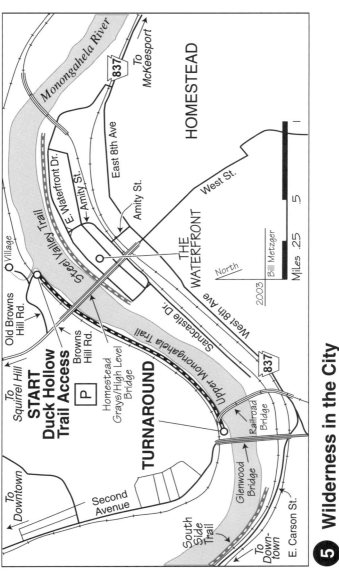

5 Wilderness in the City

#6 Steel Valley Promenade
The Waterfront in Homestead

Location:
Homestead, Allegheny County
Length: 2.3-mile round-trip
Surface: concrete sidewalks and crushed limestone
Slope: level

Select this walk to combine a short walk with shopping, dinner and, a show at The Waterfront, a shopping, dining, and entertainment center. A section of the Steel Valley Trail, this sunny, level trail provides a river walk with much to see and benches for rest stops. The Waterfront was built on the site of one of Pittsburgh's largest and most famous steel mills—The Homestead Works. Interesting industrial artifacts are positioned throughout the grounds. Embracing this heritage, The Waterfront has fashioned its logo from the twelve towering smokestacks, the most prominent remnants of the steel mill.

The Walk

To begin your walk, start at Damon's restaurant parking lot and note the towering **gantry crane**. Follow the sidewalk toward the green pedestrian bridge, make a left towards Mitchell's Fish Market onto the walkway and trail behind Mitchell's. Trim railings and gas lamps line the trail as it wanders behind restaurants along the river and under the **Homestead Grays/High Level Bridge**.

Between eateries, a **ladle car**, which once carried molten metal, decorates the trail side. A drinking fountain and benches mark a nice spot to stop and enjoy the view. Continue past office buildings, stopping at the construction area, the current end of the trail. Turn around and head back to Mitchell's Fish Market. This time, cross the green pedestrian bridge into **The Waterfront's Town Center** with its old-fashioned storefronts, brick sidewalks, hanging baskets, and boxwoods. Walk to the left past shops to another artifact, the **dinkey engine**, between Dave and Buster's and the Improv. This little engine pulled the ladle cars across the hot metal bridge.

Browse the stores before returning to your car or bus. You may decide to stay for a movie or dinner at one of the many fine restaurants in this beautiful urban shopping center.

Amenities

Here you will find just about anything you could think of: ample free parking,

The Waterfront. By AE Richardson

restaurants and eateries, shopping, entertainment, restrooms, benches, public phones, and
drinking fountains all in beautiful surround-
ings. The public restrooms are just off the
Town Center end of the pedestrian bridge.

Getting There

By Public Transit: City buses 55D, 56E, 59U
stop by Loews Theater. Cross safely to the trail
from the green pedestrian bridge in
Town Center. Check with the Port Authority
for current schedules: 412-442-2000.

By Car: From I-376 (Parkway East), take Exit 5
(Squirrel Hill/Homestead), follow signs for
Homestead, cross Hazelwood Avenue. Stay
straight to Browns Hill Road, cross the
Homestead Grays/High Level Bridge and follow
signs to The Waterfront. Make a right behind
Loews Theater to East Waterfront Drive and
cross to Damon's parking lot.

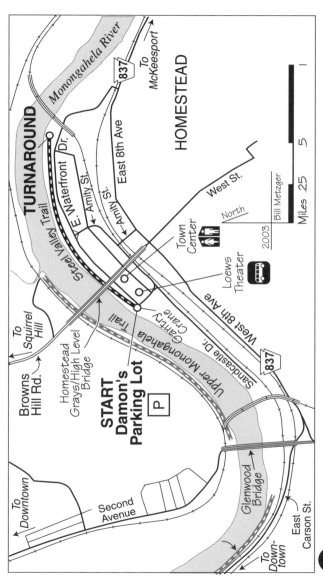

6 Steel Valley Promenade

#7 Sweet Enlow
Cliff Mine to Five Points

Location: Findlay Twp., Allegheny County
Length: 2.7-mile round-trip to tunnel or 3.8-mile round-trip to Five Points
Surface: packed stone
Slope: slight hill climbing 68 ft. in under 2 miles

Select this walk to enjoy many crossings of the meandering Montour Run and the lighted Enlow Tunnel. This walk on a sunny trail surfaced in packed crushed stone rises a moderate sixty-eight feet over 1.8 miles. Though the slope is small, it may be noticable to someone pushing a wheel-chair. You will pass wooded hillsides, rocky cliffs, and residential backyards.

The Walk

Enter the trail from the Cliff Mine parking area with Cliff Mine Road on your right. At 0.2 miles you will come to a road crossing. Exercise caution when crossing this busy road.

Along the way interpretive exhibits tell trail users about the **Stream Bank Stabilization Project**, **abandoned mine drainage**, and the benefits of **wetlands**. Bridges, benches and rock out-croppings provide pleasant spots to watch for kingfishers and wild birds. Soon **Enlow Tunnel** comes into view; walk through to the other side and note the **high rock walls** on both sides of the trail. These rocks were

One of many bridge crossings

blasted away in the 1920s, half a century into the construction of the **Montour Railroad.** Once you reach these rocks, you may turn around to complete a 2.7-mile round-trip or continue an additional 0.6 miles to Five Points and back for a 3.8-mile round-trip.

Amenities

Portable toilets can be found at the Cliff Mine parking lot and the West Ridge Ball Field at Five Points. The ball field has a drinking fountain near the backstop. At the Five Points intersection, a service station across the road has vending machines with snacks and beverages. Again, exercise caution when crossing roads. The closest restaurants are Settle Inn (297 Mahoney Road, Imperial) and Schmidt's Tavern, which is a half block from the trail access (3069 Cliff Mine Road, Clinton). Others are located at Robinson Town Center off the Parkway West.

Getting There
By Public Transit:
The 26E and 28E Moon Run/Imperial buses stop at both ends of the walk, the Cliff Mine access and Five Points. Check with the Port Authority for current schedules: 412-442-2000.

Authors' Note
Back before the days of the trail, the Montour Rail Road was the 51-mile feeder line between the two main rail lines in Clairton and Coraopolis. Trains carried coal between the mines along Montour Run and the main rail lines where the coke works were.

By Car: From Pittsburgh, take I-279S/Fort Pitt Bridge/Airport/PA-60 (Parkway West)11.8 miles, past Robinson Town Center. Take Exit 2 Montour Run Road. At the end of the ramp bear right, at traffic light turn left onto Cliff Mine Road. Follow 0.6 miles to trail access at Cliff Mine and Steubenville Pike/Enlow Road.

Montour Run Exit

Montour Run Rd.

"Parkway West"

Summit Park Dr

NORTH POINTE

60

Aten Rd.

Industry Dr.

Enlow Rd.

Cliff Mine Rd.

START
Cliff Mine
Trail Access

P

RIDC PARK

Montour Trail

North

2003

Bill Metzger

Miles .25 .5 1

Mahoney Rd.

Enlow Tunnel
575' long
(Lighted)

Montour Run

Cliff Mine Rd.

TURNAROUND
Enlow Trail
Access

P

West Ridge
Ball Field

Old Steubenville Pike

To Pittsburgh

McClaren Rd.

Enlow Rd.

West Allegheny Rd.

Imperial
Exit

22 30

US

ENLOW
(Five Points)

IMPERIAL

30

To Weirton

7 **Sweet Enlow**

#8 Walker's Mile
Walkers Mill to Gregg Station

Location: Collier Twp., Allegheny County.
Length: 4.6 miles round-trip
Surface: packed crushed stone
Slope: nearly level, slightly uphill

Select this sunny walk on the Panhandle Trail to see fascinating rock formations, rock quarries, windmills, and innovative pond aeration techniques. Only 10 miles from the heart of downtown Pittsburgh, this quiet sunny trail is a treat to explore.

The Walk

To begin, head west (toward the pavilions) on the trail from the Walkers Mill access parking lot. Crossing the first of **several bridges** over Robinson Run, you will notice tall **rock formations** to the right that are the beginning of the **quarry**.

At 0.2 miles, a **cave entrance** opens to the right. Interested in spelunking? Even though the gate may be open, you must obtain permission before entering. Contact the Collier Township at 412-279-2525.

At 0.3 miles, you come to the windmill, quarries, and a pavilion. The windmill is pumping air into the larger quarry's pond to increase its oxygen content. Oxygen reduces weed and algae growth, improves clarity, increases fish growth, eliminates odor problems, prevents summer and winter fish kill, and reduces organic bottom sediments. Compare the water of the larger quarry pond to the un-aerated smaller quarry pond.

As you go under Nike Site Road at 1.5 miles, look up on the nearby hillside and see the former installation of the **Nike missile launch sites** of the 1950s. Notice **rock formations** rising high on both sides of the trail at mile 1.9. Just after this, there's a great **overlook** where you'll get a bird's-eye view of the stream below. Conveniently, you'll also find a bench.

The **Gregg Station** (2.3 miles) trail access area is a good place to rest. You'll find a **picnic pavilion, trail information**, and **portable toilet**. Turn around at this point and return to Walkers Mill to complete the walk.

Quarry Windmill at 0.3 miles

#8 Walker's Mile

Amenities
You'll find food at Doug's Family Restaurant, two blocks from Walkers Mill access. Walkers Mill access has ample free parking, portable toilet (seasonal), trail information, picnic table, pavilion, grill, and benches. The Gregg Station trail access area has all of the above minus the grill.

Getting There
By Public Transit: The 33F McDonald services the bus stop at Noblestown and Walkers Mill Road several times a day. Check with the Port Authority for current schedules: 412-442-2000.

By Car: Begin from I-279/ US-22/US-30 (Parkway West), merge onto I-79S. Go south on I-79 toward Washington, PA, 2.08 miles. Take Exit 57 toward Carnegie. Merge right from the exit onto Noblestown Road toward Oakdale, 1.6 miles. Turn left onto Walkers Mill Road by Doug's Family Restaurant. Look for trail signs. The trail is two blocks from this intersection.

To Pittsburgh

79

Carnegie Exit 57

To Washington, PA

Robinson Run

Noblestown Rd.

North

2003

Bill Metzger

Miles   .25   .5

Doug's Restaurant

START
Walkers Mill
Trail Access

P

RENNERDALE

Walkers Mill Rd.

Noblestown Rd.

Panhandle Trail

Quary & Windmill

Hilltop Rd.

SETTLERS CABIN PARK

Overlook

Gregg Station Rd.

Nike Site Rd.

Military Reservation (Nike Site)

TURNAROUND
Gregg
Trail Access

P

Trail to McDonald

8 Walker's Mile

#9 National Tunnel
Kurnick Plot to McConnells Rd. Station

Location: Cecil Twp., Washington County
Length: 2.2-mile round-trip
Surface: packed, crushed limestone
Slope: nearly level, slightly uphill

Select this quiet, shady walk on the oldest section of the Montour Trail to see the National Tunnel. This section of the trail, paralleling McPherson Run, was completed October 10, 1992, and stretched the four miles between Cecil Park and Hendersonville. Like the trail, National Tunnel was originally built for railroad use and was later converted for trail use.

The Walk

Start at Kurnick Plot Access along Cecil-Hendersonville Road where you will find a small pavilion, picnic table, benches and nicely landscaped **flower gardens**. The bulletin board and map supply information concerning construction updates and trail news. From the parking lot, face the trail and turn right onto the trail, heading west.

It is less than one mile to the **National Tunnel**. As you approach, hillsides narrow into a heavily shaded gorge, foreshadowing the tunnel to come! There is no lighting in this **633-foot long** tunnel, which bends through the mountain at an **elevation of 1138 feet**, making the middle very dark. You may want to bring a flashlight. The tunnel is sometimes called the

Photo compliments of The Pittsburgh Post Gazette

"National Cave" in the winter because of the icy stalagmites and stalactites that form, exaggerating its cavernous appearance. The surface in the tunnel is softer ballast and has some ruts, so it can be slightly more challenging for strollers and wheelchairs. As you leave the tunnel, you'll begin the brighter portion of your walk. Continue another 0.3 miles, soaking in the sun, to McConnell Road Station, your turnaround point. When you're ready for more faux spelunking, head back through the tunnel to complete a 2.2-mile walk.

Amenities

The Kurnick access has a pavilion, picnic table, and drinking fountain, and there is a portable toilet at the McConnell access. You'll find food and beverage at Big Jim's Roadhouse (in Hendersonville on Cecil-Hendersonville Road) as well as a public phone.

Getting There
By Public Transit: None

Authors' Note
Kurnick Plot Access is a popular site for local events and was even the wedding site for two avid trail users in 1997! So keep your eyes peeled for festival flyers.

By Car: Begin from I-279/US-22/US-30 (Parkway West), merge onto I-79S via Exit 1A toward Washington, PA 10.9 miles; take Exit 48 toward Southpointe and Hendersonville. At the bottom of the ramp, follow signs to Hendersonville, turn left (east) onto Southpointe Boulevard, go 0.6 miles, then left (north) onto Morganza Road 0.5 miles, make a slight left onto Cecil-Hendersonville Road 0.9 miles. You'll see a sign for the Montour Trail before turning left into the Kurnick Plot Access where you'll find ample free parking.

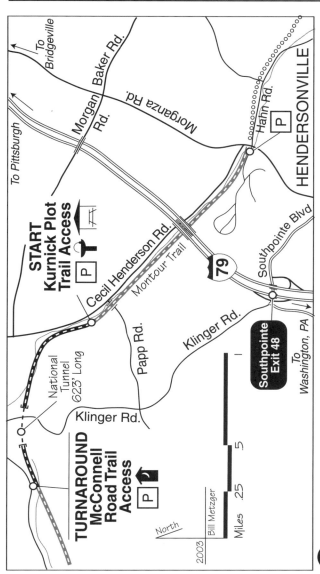

#10 Pace Peters
Arrowhead Trail

Location: Peters Twp., Washington County
Length: 6.4-mile round-trip
Surface: asphalt
Slope: nearly level, slightly uphill

The Arrowhead trail offers a little piece of serenity, weaving between residential areas, the pleasures of woods, and light commercialism. Benches, trash cans, and clean-up bags for dog waste are available at the several trail access areas along the trail.

The Walk

Start your walk at the PA-19 access. The trail only goes in one direction. Enjoy the comfortable shade of your walk by mile 0.3 as you begin to move away from the commercial atmosphere. After you cross a **wooden bridge**, your path curves with the terrain through a heavily wooded section. At 1.0 mile, the slope becomes a little more noticeable but is still quite easy to walk; if you are pushing strollers or using a wheelchair, the slope could become tiresome. Soon you will weave back out into commercial areas.

At 1.6 miles, the enchanting atmosphere of a trail-side vendor welcomes trail users with soft

Scones & Cones, a trail-side vendor

drinks, specialty coffees, teas, mulled cider, ice cream, and pastries. The **mulched outdoor seating** area is resplendent with **ivy-covered tree trunks**, **soft music**, a **trickling pond**, and **flowers**. This is also where you will find the only trail-side portable toilet on this walk. At this point, you can turn back to complete 3.2 miles, or continue through outskirts of residential and wooded areas.

If you continue, you'll traverse an excellent area for **deer watching**, especially at morning and dusk when deer come out foraging for food. If you see a deer, stay still or keep your movements slow to lengthen your encounter.

The trail access area at 2.4 miles into the walk (between 824 and 828 BeBout Road) is handicap-only and provides the best wheelchair access to the trail with space for three vehicles. This is also where an **intersecting trail** will take you to Peterswood Park. After crossing an **elevated bridge** over Sugar Camp Road, at

3.0 miles, you will see a large **horse farm** on the right. At this point, you can turn back to complete your 6.4-mile walk.

Amenities

Scones and Cones, a vendor along the trail, provides opportunity for a snack and bathroom break on the trail. Kofenya, also along the trail near the PA-19 access, is a restaurant/coffee shop/internet cafe with a public phone. This entire area is close to major roadways and an abundance of dining options. Peterswood Park, in season, provides restrooms and drinking water.

Getting There
By Public Transit: None

By Car: The trail is approximately 13 miles from the City of Pittsburgh. Take the Fort Pitt Bridge South to Exit 5A Banksville Road/PA-19S, or Liberty Bridge, follow PA-19S, through Dormont and Mt. Lebanon (which is usually very crowded with both parked and moving cars) and past South Hills Village. At 1.8 miles past Boyce Road, at the intersection of PA-19 and Valley Brook Road, make a left at the traffic light toward McMurray. At the stop sign make a right. Go under the PA-19 overpass, look for trail signs, and make a quick left into the parking lot by the Peters Township Sanitary Authority.

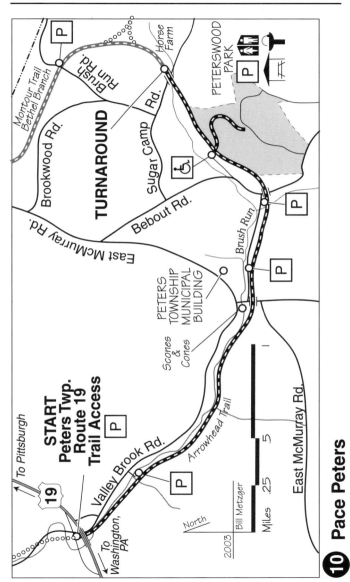

Montour Trail
Bethel Branch

P

Brush Run Rd.

Horse Farm

PETERSWOOD PARK

P

Brookwood Rd.

Sugar Camp Rd.

TURNAROUND

East McMurray Rd.

Bebout Rd.

Brush Run

P

PETERS TOWNSHIP MUNICIPAL BUILDING

P

Scones & Cones

START
Peters Twp.
Route 19
Trail Access

P

To Pittsburgh

19

Valley Brook Rd.

P

Arrowhead Trail

To Washington, PA

North

Miles   .25   .5

Bill Metzger

2003

East McMurray Rd.

❿ **Pace Peters**

#11 Haunting Beauty
Boston to Dead Man's Hollow

Location: Elizabeth Twp., Allegheny County
Length: 2.3-mile round-trip
Surface: packed, crushed limestone, mulch, gravel, dirt
Slope: nearly level, slightly uphill

Nearby towns seem miles away from this quiet, creek-side, sweet-smelling woodland trail, tucked into a hillside. Its many benches invite you to sit a spell, pause, listen, breathe, and enjoy the solitude. Take time to notice a scampering groundhog, the trill of a bird, colorful fungi growing on a log, and the trickle of a brook.

The Walk

Begin at the Boston trail access area to the Youghiogheny River Trail (YRT). The YRT's surface is wheelchair-accessible, but **Dead Man's Hollow** is not level and may have fallen trees over the path; therefore, it is not recommended for wheelchair use. With the river on your right, follow the YRT for 0.8 miles to the Dead Man's Hollow entrance. A placard displays trail maps and information.

Shortly after the entrance, the **Ruins Trail Loop** branches right; stay left on Dead Man's

Trail. Myrtle covers the ground at the far end of a **long-abandoned factory** whose roofless structure holds a picnic table. Just before you cross the creek, **Witch Hazel Trail** leads to the left. It is very steep with unstable footing, but you may want to go a short distance to see the **moss-covered steps**. While they may look natural, these steps were man-made. Backtrack to Dead Man's Trail and cross the **wooden bridge**.

Just before the halfway point, you will come to a stream which can be crossed by stepping on large rocks. Shortly, you'll come to a massive **triple-trunk sycamore tree**. The trail leading right is **Black Oak Trail**; Dead Man's continues left, looping you back toward Boston. When you return to your car, you will have completed 2.3 miles.

Triple-trunk Sycamore at trail apex

Amenities
The Boston access pro-vides free parking,

drinking fountain, portable toilets, public phone, snacks, and bike rentals. You'll find ice cream and snacks opposite the Boston Bridge. You may choose to go a short distance on East Smithfield Street to find the Boston Waterfront Restaurant with patio dining and entertainment. Pick up *The Trails of Dead Man's Hollow*, by Karen Frank, at local shops.

Getting There

By Public Transit: Gold Link Bus 60A (a Port Authority shuttle bus connecting the main line buses at the McKeesport terminal) stops at the Boston Bridge in Boston, PA. From the Boston Bridge, it's a two-block walk to the trail access. With the river on your right, follow West Smithfield Street, turn right on Donner Street to reach the trail. Check with the Port Authority for current schedules: 412-442-2000.

By Car: From Pittsburgh, take PA-51S to PA-48N (Orange Belt). Follow PA-48N for 6 to 8 miles (watching for trail access signs) to a 5-way intersection in Boston. Just before crossing the bridge, turn left onto Smithfield Street, then make a quick right onto Donner Street; trail parking is on the left.

From east of Pittsburgh take I-376 (Parkway East) or US-30E. Follow PA-48S (Orange Belt) across the Boston Bridge, and as soon as you cross the bridge make a right on to Smithfield Street, then another right on to Donner Street. Trail access parking is on the left.

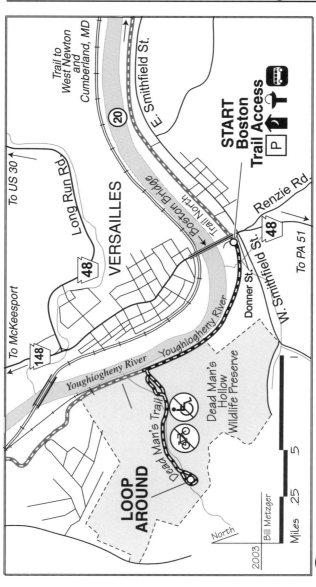

11 Haunting Beauty

#12 Old Towns & New Prairies
Sutersville to Dravo Cemetery

Location: Elizabeth Twp., Allegheny County
Length: 5.8-mile round-trip or 9.2-mile round-trip
Surface: packed, crushed limestone
Slope: level

Select this walk to experience really small town USA and open prairie. As you pass through this former coal country, you'll see evidence of its mining history. See how miners and their families lived in uniform company towns. Observe the impact this industry had on the environment at one of the largest examples of acid mine drainage in Pennsylvania, Red River Falls. This sunny walk is on part of the Youghiogheny River Trail.

The Walk to Old Towns

From the parking lot, cross the road to get to the trail. This is the first of many road crossings and the busiest, *so use caution.* Other crossings will be local roads in Blythdale, Industry, and Buena Vista. These towns, known as **coal patches** or **company towns**, are similarly built with small homes placed closely together on the banks of the river and up the hillsides. Originally, four families lived in each house—one family per corner. Notice the multiple doors. At mile 1.5 of your walk, you'll come across more evidence of this area's coal mining history: a large **red waterfall of acid mine drainage**.

Facilities at Dravo Cemetery

A church, **Bell Chapel**, is the landmark as you enter Buena Vista, where a picnic pavilion and river access await you. You may turn around at this point to complete a 5.8-mile walk. If you choose to continue, it is 2 miles more to Dravo Cemetery.

The Walk to New Prairies

After Buena Vista, the trail opens up to a prairie with broad, flat areas between the trail and river. At **Dravo Cemetery** (4.6 miles), a pavilion now stands where a church was once destroyed by fire, rebuilt, and burned again. Today, just the graveyard remains. Gravestones bear the names of early settlers, nine **Civil War** veterans and one **War of 1812** veteran. Majestic, gnarled maple trees border a path leading to a **primitive campground** and river view. Some campers will swear the cemetery is haunted. Turn around here to complete 9.2 miles.

> ## Authors' Note
> It is believed that Queen Aliquippa, the leader of a local Native American tribe in the 1700s, had her summer village between Buena Vista and Dravo Cemetery. Her loyalty to George Washington and the British is legendary.

Amenities
The access area has free parking, portable toilet, and an information board. At McPherson Street and Douglas Run Road, a gas station and a Tastee Freez provide food, drink, ice cream, and a pay phone. Across from the Buena Vista pavilion, you'll find soft drink vending machines. Dravo Cemetery facilities include a permanent restroom, picnic pavilion, and old-fashioned water pump.

Getting There
By Public Transit: None

By Car: The Sutersville trail access area is 22 miles from downtown Pittsburgh. Take PA-51S toward Uniontown for 16 miles. Turn left onto PA-48. You will drive through a valley. At the top of the second hill will be a four-way intersection. Make a right onto Round Hill Road. After 2.8 miles, Round Hill Road ends and you will merge left onto Douglas Run Road. Watch for blue and white YRT signs marking the Sutersville access area at the intersection of Douglas Run Road and McPherson Street.

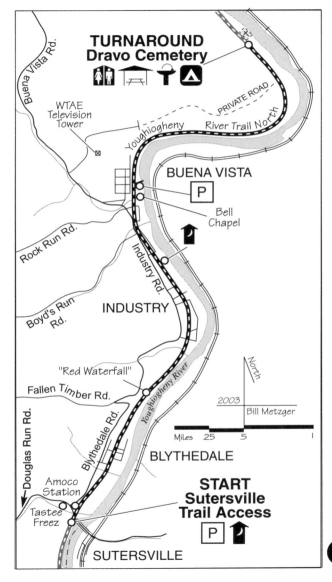

TURNAROUND
Dravo Cemetery

Buena Vista Rd.

WTAE
Television
Tower

PRIVATE ROAD

Youghiogheny   River Trail North

BUENA VISTA

P

Bell
Chapel

Rock Run Rd.

Industry Rd.

INDUSTRY

Boyd's Run
Rd.

"Red Waterfall"

Fallen Timber Rd.

Youghiogheny River

North

2003   Bill Metzger

Miles   25   5   1

Douglas Run Rd.

Blythedale Rd.

BLYTHEDALE

Amoco
Station

Tastee
Freez

START
Sutersville
Trail Access

P

SUTERSVILLE

12 Old Towns & New Prairies

The Trail System

The trails in this book were built and are being maintained by public entities, trail organizations, and volunteers. Trail contact information is listed in the next section.

You will be walking mainly on sections of the Great Allegheny Passage, the longest multi-purpose rail-trail in the East. When finished, the Passage will stretch 150 non-motorized, nearly-level miles from Pittsburgh, PA to Cumberland, MD, with a 52-mile spur to Pittsburgh International Airport. Currently, 100 continuous miles are open from McKeesport, PA to near Meyersdale, PA, plus several smaller segments in Pittsburgh. The Passage will join the C&O Canal Towpath in Cumberland to expand the off-road trail linkage to Washington, DC.

Designated a National Recreation Trail, the Passage enables people to hike, bike, or cross-country ski, discovering quaint towns and scenic river gorges using the railroad engineering expertise of massive bridges and tunnels to pass through the Allegheny Mountains.

The Allegheny Trail Alliance (ATA) is a coalition of trail groups building the Passage. ATA is: Friends of the Riverfront, Steel Valley Trail Council, Montour Trail Council, Regional Trail Corporation, DCNR—Ohiopyle State Park, Somerset Rails-to-Trails Association, and Allegheny Highlands Trail of MD.

Great Little Walks Contact Information

For many of these walks, there are multiple sources for more information. Thus, you'll find the walks listed more than once below.

Great Allegheny Passage

(Walks # 2, 3, 4, 6, 7, 9, 11, 12)

Allegheny Trail Alliance

419 College Avenue
Greensburg, PA 15601
888-282-2453 (888-ATA-BIKE)
atamail@atatrail.org
www.atatrail.org

Three Rivers Heritage Trail

(Walks # 1, 2, 3, 4, 5)

City of Pittsburgh

Office of the Mayor
5th Floor-City County Bldg.
414 Grant Street
Pittsburgh, PA 15219
412-255-2626
www.city.pittsburgh.pa.us

Three Rivers Heritage Trail

(Walks # 1, 2, 3, 4)

Friends of the Riverfront

P.O. Box 42434
Pittsburgh, PA 15203
412-488-0212
www.friendsoftheriverfront.org

Steel Valley Trail
(Walk # 6)
Steel Valley Trail Council
P.O. Box 318
Homestead, PA 15120
412-225-2530
Hannah.Ehrlich@city.pittsburgh.pa.us
www.steelvalleytrail.org.

Montour Trail
(Walks # 7, 8, 9, 10)
Montour Trail Council
P.O. Box 11866
Pittsburgh, PA 15228
412-831-2030
info@montourtrail.org
www.montourtrail.org

Panhandle Trail
(Walk # 8)
Collier Township
2814 Hilltop Road
Presto, PA 15142
412-276-5051
www.panhandletrail.org

Arrowhead Trail
(Walk # 10)
Peters Township
Eddie Figas, Director
200 Municipal Drive
McMurray, PA 15317
724-942-5000
etfigas@peterstownship.com

Dead Man's Hollow
(Walk # 11)
Allegheny Land Trust
1901 Glen Mitchell Road
Sewickley, PA 15143
412-749-4882
www.alleghenylandtrust.org

Youghiogheny River Trail North
(Walks # 11, 12)
Regional Trail Corporation
P.O. Box 95
West Newton, PA 15089
724-872-5586
yrt@westol.com
www.youghrivertrail.com

Helpful Websites
These sites offer tips on getting the maximum
benefit from your walks.

Jewish Healthcare Foundation Working,
   Hearts Program, www.workinghearts.org

Center for Healthy Aging,
   www.healthyaging.pitt.edu

Public Broadcasting Systems,
   www.pbs.org/americaswalking

Johnson Foundation Active Living Program,
   www.rwjf.org/programs/physicalActivity.jsp

Partnership for Prevention, www.prevent.org

Legend

 Bicycles

 Wheelchair Accessible

Amenities

P Parking

 Food Near Trail

 Restrooms

 Portable toilet

 Public Phone

 Drinking Fountain

 Picnic Pavilion

 Camping

 Picnic Tables or Benches

Transportation

 Port Authority Bus

 "T" Light Rail

Great Little Walk

Other Trail

T Line

Highway

Railroad

Stream